LOVE, PAIN, & GLORY: REDEMPTION

LEO JAMES

Acknowledgements

All praise and glory go to GOD. Thank you, Lord, for blessing me with, now, two sons Noble and Kawhi. They've been my greatest motivation throughout this journey. I want you both to know I did this for us and the youth of future generations. I'd like to thank my beautiful queen and soulmate, Lovanda. Thank you for being my Superwoman, true motivator, and supporter.

You are the definition of a PHENOMENAL WOMAN. Thank you, mom, dad, Frankie, and Corey for being there for me during one of the lowest points of my life. You all came together to epitomize the true definition of family.

And of course, a special thank you to all who have supported me on this journey of Love, Pain, & Glory. I encourage you all to apply my vision of empowering the youth in your daily approach. They are, after all, our future. And for those who left me, refused to support, or doubted my vision, thank you. Your absence and apathy fueled this initiative, and I pray for you all with gratitude.

Love and Blessings,

Leo James

Table of Contents

DADDY'S PAL 7

MY SON 13

YOURS TRULY 15

SONS 2 SUNS 18

KAWHI 20

BROTHER'S KEEPER: 23

NOBLE & KAWHI 23

DEEP THOUGHTS 26

REDEMPTION 36

RESURRECTION 39

WALKING TESTIMONY 42

SUPERIOR 44

FACE 47

MOMENT TO PRAY	50
HAND 2 HAND	53
THE STATE VS LEO JAMES	55
TIME WILL RIGHT THE WRONGS	61
HEAR TO ENLIGHTEN	63
LAST KISS	67
SONS 2 SUNS	69
INVOLUNTARY FIGHT	71
KING AND QUEEN	73
QUEEN/SOULMATE	78
BOOK LOVE	80
THE MOMENT	83
DI PREE	87
STEPPING OUT THE GAME	90

MINE	94
-WITH LOVANDA BROWN	94
COUPLES THERAPY	99
CHANCE	103
BLACKED OUT	106
DOWN AND UP	108
LAW OF ATTRACTION	110
GROWTH	113
THE RESOLVE	116
HEAR ME SAVE YOU	118
ONLY THE BEGINNING	121
PLEASE READ	123
STORY	126
THE GREATEST	128

CELEBRATE	132
GOD IS MY JUDGE	134
GOD IS MY GLORY	137
SPOTLIGHT	139
PROPHECY	141
MADE IT	143
MY EVERYTHING	146
P.R.E.V.A.I.L 4	149
"WHY P.R.E.V.A.I.L 4"	149

Daddy's Pal

I've learned that it's hard to hold back tears when you feel something so deeply that it touches your soul. I sit back and remember the day I was informed that I was going to be a dad. My son's mother was on a cruise eating and sleeping a lot. That was a sign that she was pregnant. I didn't pay much attention because it was all words. I smiled and cried once the pregnancy test showed two lines. Those two lines were as clear as day. It all came together like street lines or a railroad track. I did everything I could do to prepare for my new blessing. I still recall going to the doctors to reveal the gender. I was praying for a boy. Once I seen the private thumbs up and the word boy across the monitor screen, I smiled and pumped my fist with excitement. I made sure my son's mom had every craving desired. I still recall driving all the way from Connecticut to New York to BBQ's just for some honey glazed chicken wings. I was upset at first, but I smile just thinking about it because I was willing to do any and everything for my Prince. I remember rubbing his mom's belly to his movement. I spoke to him as if I was giving a motivational speech. My voice and his movement automatically put a smile on me and his mother's face.

Fast asleep but woke up to a phone call saying, "my water broke." I thought I was dreaming at first but then came to realization after looking at the time. I had to wake up in a few hours, anyway for school and work. I was smiling ear to ear. I was nervous because I didn't know what to expect. They said don't eat before labor, but we went to IHOP that morning and had a feast. The nickname "Munch" came from his mom having many cravings and running up my money. Eating something here and there. His mom was stuck at 8 cm dilated, so she had a c-section. Since I was a new dad, I was filled with mixed emotions. We decided together that the name Noble was best. As the woman and mother of the child, she was given the opportunity to pick who she wanted to be in the room. She decided to pick her mom. I felt slighted because that was *my* son, but I understood where she came from. She felt more comfortable with her mom and now I see why. Her mom is the one that will always be around through right or wrong. I cried like a baby knowing that I was the dad but had to sit out in the waiting area. I felt a little at ease when her mom came out and stated that he looked like my sister. I smiled and was ready to see him for the first time. I thought to myself like God knew what was going on. It's remarkable how his expected due date was my sister's birthday, but he came out a day before.

My heart melted when I saw my son for the first time. I held him in my hands as I shed tears of joy. I didn't want to let him go. I loved him up with kisses. I used to always get nervous holding my nephews and nieces, but there's no better feeling than holding something that you can say is yours forever. I love kids with a passion and always wanted my own, so it's worth saying that my son was planned, and I prepared myself to be one of the best dads in the world. That journey started as we left the hospital on a snowy day. I'm typically a chill guy, but I must admit my anxiety levels were out of the roof as I placed my son in the car seat. As I drove away from the hospital, I felt goosebumps and a taste of reality settling in. I don't mind pressure moments, but my new life was about to be filled with a lot of crying, fatigue, and extreme parenting. For example, I was waking up about 2 or 3 times in the morning to change diapers, feed, or just hold my little me for comfort. There were times when my son's mom would lie and say that she got up and tended to him. She will then go back to sleep which forced me to wake up and tend to him. Keep in mind that I still had to wake up to work and go to school. It was really challenging. I honestly did more than the average man is supposed to. It's supposed to be a 50-50 split, but I felt like I did it all. I strongly believe if most men had to do what I was doing, they would choose to have only one kid and that's the truth. It's no way you can do all of that and still manage to have more kids. A true dedicated man isn't just going to have more kids knowing that he's doing most of the work such as waking up, changing diapers, and etc. It makes sense that most men have all these kids because they know and will leave the woman to handle majority of the work. I've learned that a child deserves their parents all.

Speaking about doing it all, yes, I was forced to do it all when my son's mother cheated on me. I was forced to cook, clean, pay bills, work, and take care of my son for the times I had him. This experience made me really respect all of the single parents out there giving it their all. It's not easy, whatsoever, but I made it work. I made that experience worthwhile, and my son and I were able to build an unbreakable bond. I'm a huge advocate for education so we tend to and still do educational activities such as counting, writing, and reading. We also were able to play video games and do a lot of activities such as bike riding, soccer, football, basketball, and everything else that might come to mind. Through all of this, my ultimate goal was to raise a boy into a man. I've been instilling discipline through vigorous activities. I taught him how to take responsibility and accountability. I wanted him to understand being a black man comes with a lot and that he will have to work twice as hard than the next man. I wanted him to know that there's a lesson in everything that we do. Through the midst of everything being taught, I taught him to have self-respect and respect for others to get him further in life. I've planted each seed of **P.R.E.V.A.I.L** which are *purpose, respect, education, vision, attitude, inspire*, and *leadership* in his life since birth. "Daddy you're the king of P.R.E.V.A.I.L," he would say. One day the torch will be passed to him as he will be in position to enlighten others with all the knowledge and wisdom he's inherited over the years. That's the very day that he will live up to his name and show the world who's **Noble.**

My Son

Twenty-Twenty won, but best believe I'm not done.

Redemption is here but I experienced a long run.

I'm on a mission to give my all to my son.

I got the world on my shoulders so I'm lifting a ton.

I'm built for it

You'll never see me quit.

Mind over matter and I know my purpose

so I'm sticking to the script.

Daddy got some big shoes to feel.

I know you look up to me like Shaq.

The man of steel.

I'm always by your side

like we're playing the video game.

I see you throwing up the X.

They can't hold you

as you dominate every football game.

We put the work in every time we train.

Pay attention to those who are planning to jump the train.

I instilled so many jewels in your heart

in which it will shine like a chain.

Have fun but get the job done like balling in the rain.

My job as a dad is to show you what this life is about.

Love, Pain, and Glory

for you to see and feel what I write about.

This is our journey to P.R.E.V.A.I.L

so get ready as we ride it out.

Yours Truly

Pen in my right hand
Writing down my thoughts
For you to truly understand.
Tears falling down my eyes
As I think about you 24/7
Praying to God
To get you back by my side.
I feel the pain
And it feels as if I'm dying.
Some say men aren't supposed to cry
I'll tell you right now
They're lying.
I feel the love
so that's why it's hard to stop crying.
I know you're hurt too.
Being separated is not what we're used to.

I'm coming back stronger.

I promise to make it up to you.

I'm on a mission to get you back.

I'm building myself up and what I lack.

I've struggled but I can't blame it on the pandemic.

My vision getting clearer.

High definition, best believe it's dynamic.

Not having you by my side

Is like I lost a rib.

Daddy's Pal is what I see as I hold your bib.

I'm reflecting on life and all the what if's

Man's Search for Meaning

was my journey, you can call this.

The love and pain feelings are so deep.

Thinking about you so many nights

to where I was tossing and turning in my sleep.

The moment we reunite

is when the dark clouds turn to sunshine light.

Our time away was a part of our story.

God allowed us to experience the love and pain

To truly appreciate and feel the

Glory!

Sons 2 Suns

When you'd see me and my son—
that was my identifier
Redemption was already prepared by God
to be placed in the air fryer.
I kept it all the way real—
never wanted to be a liar.
No need for that, lessons learned
Like a pinky promise and shoes being tied.
Dry eyed but
Every time I thought everything through,
It led to several moments in which I cried.
I'm still alive but away from you.
Hoping you don't think of me as if I died.
Praying the things I taught resonated.
When it came to raisin' you in the sun
Challenges like life's showers,

I never hesitated.

You've seen me do it alone

and now you get to see me with

a queen I'm blessed I dated.

She's been a true rider through storms

While carrying our son.

I feel true unconditional love

Through the air like a heaven-sent dove.

To you my son and my other son,

being together brings happiness

that lights a smile up brighter than the sun.

KAWHI

Unexpected but reality hit.

Mommy knew we hit big.

With you being our jack pot,

I needed time to embrace

The million dollars bundle worth of joy.

At the time was a lot

Daddy just needed time for the truth to resonate.

No greater feeling than discovering a young king

coming into the world

and hearing your due date.

Your place in our hearts leave no

Questions like why

Your mom and I made a powerful move

to get you

Like what the Spurs did to get Kawhi

So Kawhi is the name that we gave you.

I vow to be the greatest dad in the world

as I raise you.

After feeling every moment

From a row to a kick

Your mom and I are anxious

To meet our first-round pick

Your presence has strengthened our relationship,

Your arrival will help solidify our championship

Mommy and I are excited to receive our rings

Together we stand as a family,

1 queen and 3 kings.

This journey wouldn't have been

the same without you.

Through all the Love, Pain, and Glory.

God Blessed us to P.R.E.V.A.I.L forward

And therefore

Kawhi Leo James,

WE LOVE YOU!

Brother's Keeper:
NOBLE & KAWHI

I'm starting off with

I love you

My two sons.

It was written

For this journey

That I'm now done.

I'm looking forward

To having fun

during times like breakfast and lunch,

bonding at the park

Me, Popa, and Munch.

Always be a brother's keeper

Expect the unexpected

Get all non-believers

To become believers.
Know that I'm raising Kings
To be givers
And not receivers
Through thick and thin
No matter what
Hold each other down.
These are my spoken words
just in case I'm not around.
Respect your mom and others,
just prepare to be the man,
Don't be afraid to handle situations
You are your fathers' child
So I know you can.
I always say we only leave our legacy
and kids,
anything less, God always forbids.
Make sure you both try to see eye to eye

You both are black men dealing with a world

Filled with others giving privilege

So live up to your names my sons,

Noble and Kawhi

Life is all about growth,

I plan to be the greatest dad ever,

That's my written and spoken oath.

Once again, I love you both!!!

Deep Thoughts

I wrote this with the thoughts of my son

I was walking through the journey, but I had to run.

Scared for me and my son's life,

Maybe I should have just put the gun down,

and let them take me out and be a Martyr man.

In position to make a difference,

I'm extremely confident that I can.

Trusting in the system, I promise they won't understand.

Think about it once you're woke and forced to stand.

They already judging you knowing you're a black man.

They're going to understand P.R.E.V.A.I.L

and God's plan.

Best believe they're going to let you go and keep hope.

M&M, they're going to keep you in the scope

Have to be like J Cole and do what you have to do.

Every book is A-plus

Take them back to school

and put the work in while being a teacher first

Then become a Master

Journey like the marathon continues

will have you working faster.

I'd sacrificed without knowing but I couldn't

leave my son to be a bastard.

Motivational speaker speaking like a pastor.

I found my queen along the way while I'm fighting to get him back

which happened to be after.

Felt like Kawhi the Claw

one year with the Raptors.

You're coming back home

to the love and gifts.

Have to always focus on the "now' and not the "what ifs"

Daddy of the year still going for my ring

Last name James, so you know we were born to be King.

I have to make up for lost time.

Daddy and son time guaranteed

which will be bonding overtime.

They say time heals all wounds

Daddy had to feel young again

to escape reality at times and watch cartoons.

I can hear you saying now

"Daddy really?"

I miss you brightening up my days

with your smile, sense of humor,

and just being silly.

I knew you would stay strong since you're an Aquarius,

charismatic and hilarious.

Minor Setback 4 a Major Comeback

"Aye yo, I'm slipping and I'm falling, I can't get up. Get me back on my feet, so I can tear shit up." These lyrics are from the great hip hop artist DMX. These lyrics stuck with me because it displays a man who's admitting to his struggles. I've learned throughout my life that we all will struggle in some manner. Life will knock us down and as the saying goes, "it's not how we get knocked down but how we get back up." 2020 was a tough year for the whole world dealing with a global pandemic, other personal issues aside. I personally experienced a life-changing event. I've realized how someone's life can change within a blink of an eye. This just means that it only takes a few seconds. I've never gotten into trouble with the law throughout the course of my 29 years of living on this earth. Exactly 7 days before I entered my 30th chapter, I'm in handcuffs behind a police cruiser. They say you're innocent until proven guilty; I've experienced the opposite: *guilty until proven innocent.* Bail was set high, but I give thanks to my dad and brother for coming together to bail me out. It was a good thing I contacted my dad during the incident in which he rushed to my apartment to stand with me on the scene. If I hadn't contacted him, then I am confident I would have been locked up longer. My dad and my mom, who typically reaches out to me daily, would have been concerned, I am sure. Considering questions like: *"why isn't he responding?"* or *"why is his phone going straight to voicemail?"* Moments like these which help me to understand the importance of communicating with those who you care for and who cares about you daily. If they don't respond, then that's an alert to contact them and figure out what's going on. That ride in the cop cruiser alone was a time to reflect and think about life. In that moment, I felt I was betrayed by the system that was designed to protect the community. I was asked to take my du-rag off which I had on my head at the time. They cut the string out of my shorts and collected my phone, wallet, and key to my apartment. They took my picture and threw me in a cell with people who were incoherent and experienced that situation potentially more than once. The cell was small with a toilet and sink with an ineffective plumbing system. Given the pandemic at hand, I was startled and disheartened by the absence of hygiene and Covid-19 protocols in place to protect the human beings, I mean, "inmates" to ensure everyone's safety. "I'm going to fucking complain to the state about the conditions of this place," my cellmate expressed. "I'm going to shut this motherfucker down." I could understand his frustration. I witnessed injustices firsthand throughout my limited stay. If you were thirsty, then you had to ask the officers who would catch attitudes for simple requests such as these. Yes, I was met with scorn and distaste for asking the following: "can I please have my sheets and a blanket." There were many of times in which they forgot the inmates request. As if all of this weren't enough to break me, I was horrified by what I experienced next—*impromptu screams*. All I could here were fellow human beings affectionately named "inmates" yelling and screaming in pain; the isolation forcing them to hold detailed dialogue with *themselves.* You don't understand crazy until you get there. I was freezing and thinking to myself that I failed. They served you bologna and cheese sandwiches with an orange squeezing drink. They allow you to make one phone call while timing you. The call which was afforded delivered an unspoken message— "call who you can to bail yourself out." That entire experience made me feel like an animal in a cage. I thought to myself that my 29 years of existence on this earth was filled with plenty of accomplishments and accolades. All that didn't matter in the moment, so I was portrayed as a criminal. There didn't seem to be pondering thoughts of intent—that this man was just protecting himself from harm. They heard one side of the story and ran with it. It was just another black man committing a crime. They even put a protective order in place, which was the most devastating part. I was legally being kept from seeing my very own son. Can you imagine? Having raised him in your own hand and having been present since day one, and one completely misconstrued event denying you of your **RIGHT** to be with the very human you've helped create? Missing Thanksgiving, Christmas, his birthday—all holidays I've worked tirelessly to make special and memorable for the little boy who held my face and carried my blood through his veins. You're all stopping me from seeing *him?* It would have been appreciated if I was at least able to receive supervised visitation just to see, counsel and converse with my son during those times. With time passing, I've since relented to the idea of even a facetime call as being sufficient. But alas, this is not how the system was designed. Whether physically imprisoned or not, it is designed to break your psyche in the most torturous ways possible.

Just the same, they haven't succeeded. And they won't. I've never, before this, subscribed to the system and they won't solicit me today. That is my word.

One thing about redeeming oneself, the act alone has a propensity to generate a wide audience of those who've wronged you or misjudged your very purpose. Redemption is here. Thank you all for tuning in.

Redemption

Fall down, bounce back.
Sometimes it be like that.
Look around, you can see
who really has your back.
Make one decision then they
judge you based off that.
They heard the story
but still don't have all the facts.
They believe the history
all based off artifacts.
Those won't understand
unless they were a part of the plan.
Locked me up but at the end
I'm still God's chosen man.
Came back,
still on my journey to P.R.E.V.A.I.L.

Had a shortcoming event

I must admit I failed.

But I'm still on board

because the ship never sailed.

I got my captain on the boat

I swear to God she's the G.O.A.T.

Greatest of All Time

Just a breakdown

for the simple mind.

She pushes me forward

but my mind still pushing rewind.

That's when we clash

due to the backlash.

She sat me down in position

and promised me that we won't crash.

We're doing everything together.

Even stacking cash.

When it comes to these words,

I'm present and I swear I'm so gifted.

My words remove dark clouds that's been lifted.

Take a look into my eyes,

you'll see I'm prolific like Nip.

Face of P.R.E.V.A.I.L

I hope you understand the drip.

I throw my 7 up

but I promise I won't quit.

037 is unique and legit.

Living backwards but I know you're getting it.

Redemption is the end

of the Love, Pain, and Glory journey.

The Glory is what we praise.

I introduced myself, shed my last tears,

But this is the last phase!

Resurrection

I've resurrected.

Overcame the impossible and did what was unexpected.

I stayed on God's appointed journey despite being rejected.

Religious and spiritual beliefs, I'm eclectic.

Fulfilling my purpose while overcoming many fears.

Love, Pain, and Glory had me in search for freedom.

From my introduction to my Last Tears.

Now I feel complete with Redemption.

Free will from my pursuit of happiness.

God giving me an exemption

Which felt like an extension

From events which resulted in so much tension.

Found and lost myself in order to find my true self

While crying out for help to get un-invited attention.

I was writing on several walls.

Don't expect anyone to catch you after several falls.

Don't be upset when you fall hard and get several calls.

Just juggle things in life as if your hands have several balls.

Acknowledge the glass half full instead half empty.

Freedom comes when your mind and heart full of fears is completely empty.

Let go and let God take you all the way.

It was all a part of the plan when you went astray

to put all your faith in God and pray.

I remained braved on the journey that was paved.

I couldn't help save anyone if I wasn't saved.

Now that I'm resurrected with errors in my life corrected.

I was giving time to meditate on my purpose as I reflected.

Now my head is up high as I'm erected.

My words coming to life as I ejaculate.

"One of the Greatest Motivation Speakers"

If you struggled somehow, then I know you can relate.

Resurrection was a true divine fate.

Walking Testimony

As I look far, far away

Deep into the future.

The future is bright like the light of dawn

opening up to start its day.

Working like a slave on the journey

with some quality time to play.

A struggle is temporary

unless one wants it to stay.

I'm that son that shines and want everything

to feel my presence and grow from my essence.

I never knew consequences come from sequels.

If I had known, then I could have prepared

for the calm before the storm.

But with the help and guidance of faith

I was able to weather the storm.

God knew what was best, so it was

a matter of time for answered prayers.

God is our provider and protector

who guides us through all scares.

For me, it was catching me from my Last Tears.

Truth is that God always care and will always be there

through the bad and the good.

If you truly believe

then you wouldn't need to knock on wood.

Just be patient in the midst of feeling lost and misunderstood.

Walk with faith instead of fear.

Walk in faith instead of fear.

Walk within every step of faith

and dismiss any fear on your journey.

Walking testimony!

Superior

I've been through a lot, but prayers always got me through

Don't forget to give thanks to those who looked out for you.

Love or be loved, its options for you to pick and choose.

Fear or be feared, it's a difference between the two.

But fear can get you caught up.

I know we all been there too.

Make a choice but don't let the choice make you.

Because if you're not strong enough,

mentally and physically, it might just break you.

That's the time you might just surrender your soul,

by putting your hands up

or waving the white flag.

you know that's a go

They say it's a no-go when there's a no-show

but don't let other people's presence dictate your flow

with that being said, the show must go on.

Keep pushing even when they think something is wrong.

Keep your integrity and composure to display

that everything is right.

Everything in the dark always comes to the light.

Adversity will try to trip you up

but stand your ground and put up a fight.

The Art of Balance is real

and you'll always learn from that tipping point.

Life is full of highs and lows,

Family and foes,

Yes and no's,

It's not always about what you know

but who you know.

As a writer and motivational speaker, I touched so many areas

Speaking out loud with words, it's like a form of hysteria.

But when you recognize that you're in control,

It's only the way of the superior.

FACE

I tried to stop there with, "The Last Tears"

God and my family told me keep going

That's why Redemption is here.

I hit the ground hard when I fell

Middle fingers up, at the moment didn't care

Another testimony that God wanted me to share

Sitting in the cell, it was dirty with a smell

Using my shirt to keep me warm, it was cold as hail

3 days in like a block period waiting for the bail

Thoughts running through my mind

Far from P.R.E.V.A.I.L

Shaking my head in disbelief,

Like damn I failed

One day, I'll get more detailed

Just know I didn't eat nor sleep well.

Seen a few people who was probably shocked to see me

Kept my head down just hoping they didn't notice me

I told myself straight up, I'm not coming back here

If I do, it will be through my words speaking or flying a kite there

I shouldn't have been there in the first place

But I believe God had me experience that firsthand

To lift me in position and guide me to first place.

I know I will lead the way for the youth with my voice and face

Challenges came my way, but I was ready to face it

My journey has shown many times—I could have quit.

Quitting is never an option, so I trusted the process.

Face whatever you have to and believe it will lead to success.

Success doesn't happen overnight

A masterpiece could potentially be put together in one day or night.

But double up the work throughout the days and nights.

Going up against your fears will be one of the toughest fights.

I came out of it, but I faced a black eye.

On top of that, can't forget I'm a black guy.

I was well-protected, but they caught me off guard

I've always been a helping hand so you can accept my face card.

Moment to Pray

Love, Pain, and Glory: The Last Tears

Big bro came over to check up me upstairs

I told him, "Sit back" as he heard what I read

He was thinking deep while his eyes were blood shot red

I told him that I'm done, bro said "no, you're not"

I closed my laptop because at the time I was closing up shop.

Then he told me, "Bro, it's redemption time."

I apologize for leaving you son during that short period of time.

I was forced to spend some alone time to clear my mind.

Have to move forward, at any moment can't press rewind.

It hurt but I try not to question God why.
Mind was floating like a butterfly.
While getting hit with many legal fees.
Felt like I was being stung by several bees.
When it comes to the system
It's like money grow on trees.

Court dates getting pushed back
To the mind it's a tease.
Praying to God to get me through the storm.
On my hands and knees begging God please!

I thank my bro and dad
who came to bail me out
and for checking on me daily.
Phones calls or just hanging out.
It means a lot to my heart

That's why I wrote about it not knowing
where to start.

Word is bond so in due time

I'm going to pay you both back.

I know you both told me it was cool

And that I don't have to do that.

I'm about to make powerful moves.

Chip on my shoulders with a lot to prove.

I'm just awaiting that moment when I'm
approved.

They say your story shouldn't be told but sold.

I'm doing both and God is leading the way.

I shared my Love, Pain, and Glory with the
world,

so I don't have much left to say.

Just a moment to pray!

Hand 2 Hand

One foot in front of the other

That's walking the tight rope

We all trip and fall at times.

So we just need a hand of hope.

The fall can be minor or severe

but it's always how we get back up and persevere.

Through a minor setback, comes a major come back.

Trip leaving the block, hold it down while in your own lane

but staying on track

It might cause a little delay but stay on course so you're

prepared to pick up or pass the baton like a relay.

One hand washes the other

So it's only right that we support and help one another,

We who do good deeds get satisfaction

from fulfilling other's needs.

No need for anything in return that's the policy.

It be done with ease pure modesty.

This is from a giver's mindset and philosophy.

The State vs Leo James

I know I left but I'm coming back.

I fell off but God put me right back on track.

Guidance in my life for the moment

It broke my heart when I had to pack.

Tears falling once again from my eyelids.

Experience is the greatest teacher so

Lessons learned can be shared for our kids.

I must admit, it was a lot to handle

and it's hard to see clear when you're in it,

but I just kept pushing and refused to back down and submit.

Going through the storm filled with dark clouds

and precipitation is hard to predict.

The blueprint was always in God's hands

so I trust the process and knew God

all along knew the final verdict.

I sat back and observed how the system is flawed,

but the animal instinct in me kept me fighting as I stayed sharp-clawed.

The youth needs me so it's only right

to be pointed in the right direction.

Right hand up quick as if I'm in class

Ready to answer a question.

Never tended to hurt anyone.

Heart beating fast and felt under attack

so I resorted to my own protection.

I still can't believe I was treated

like a criminal with no criminal record when I obliged

by the law and didn't flee.

29 years of being a law-abiding citizen

with a resume that differentiate me from most men.

Extraordinary dad with pictures and videos as proof.

I know good people who's been taken out

which was probably investigated

and brushed under the rug with no proof.

Stood up for myself and was knocked down.

Still have love for my city and town.

It could have been worse, and I could have been

lost and found with funeral arrangements

to put me in the ground.

But I'm still here to speak and do what I do best.

P.R.E.V.A.I.L got me through the test.

Now I can be alive as I sleep peacefully and rest.

Put me in position again and ask everyone about me—

How I feel about my youth and my son.

The judge will be easily convinced

Knowing that my mission isn't done.

I fled for a better living with my Queen

in which we both like to give with

an open hand because we enjoy giving.

My dad was around side by side with her

as they both were ready for anything to occur.

God allowed me to prepare my team together

for what's ahead.

I promise to make a difference for my family, youth, and community

before I'm dead.

I witness the before, during, and after.

I'm a writer expressing myself with free writing as a drafter.

Writing is one of the greatest times for one to really feel free.

Before my son turned 7, I missed

Thanksgiving, Christmas, and his birthday.

With optimism I had all his gifts

left feeling lonely like me under the tree.

They say crime pays but is that true or is that

what people who consistently commit crimes say?

Imagine having a set date but it feels like

a waste of a day.

Ready to P.R.E.V.A.I.L

But learned that the system is designed to play.

I stayed patient but was hurting deep inside

like those trips with my hands together tied

on that rocky ride.

Mug shot with my face book

but all my words written define my life

in every book.

Connecticut born and raised.

Glory to touch my own and every other state

With God who I've always trust and praised.

Time Will Right the Wrongs

Focus on yourself and not the clock

Always stay solid like a cold rock

Make your moves without a sound

Keep working even when no ones' around

It's imperative that you change the narrative

You're a writer and a poet of your life story

Don't get too caught up in HIStory and neglect your own story.

They say two wrongs don't make it right

but we pray that a wrong turn can show

us who left and how to get our life right

Understand the power of words and why people write

Take that leap of faith with no thoughts of height

The future can be uncertain at times

but keep faith through life's darkness of uncertainty and say "Let there be light"

The time is now so don't worry about right or wrong

A journey is always long

A day will always come after night

And a sun will always come after rain

Trust that love can help overcome pain

Don't allow your past to force you to live in vain

Life will remind you that memories remain

Time heals all wounds when everything is finished

Love and Glory will outshine all the pain inside, in due time will become diminished.

Hear to Enlighten

We all take a couple bad turns
but never settle for dead ends.
Turn back around right away
Even if it means leaving behind
some family and friends.
It's just one's life purpose while GPS is
redirecting but to some it's a shame.
Focus on self in those situations and
don't think about who's to blame
Trust the process and strive to be
the winner of the game.
Break the cycle so it's not the same.
Remain focus on your main prize.
Put in the work and the results will pay off
to where you wouldn't even realize.
God gave us 2 ears and 1 mouth for a reason.
Deaf now, but you'll hear me when it's your season.

Movin' On Up

Get the facts from the horse's mouth
Some things are deeply rooted
like family ties from the south.
Representing me but low-key felt the jab
Let's be honest, some just have the Gift of Gab
They can be well spoken
But check my yearbook
I was "Most Outspoken"
Learned even saying less is more
Word-of-mouth made me fall for the allure
Knew what you was doing? Still not sure
Texts still in store, felt like I had to stalk
Wish you knew
your intentions speak before you even talk
Too bad- bro too focused on his walk
Eyes below the brim of all his cap

Couldn't even see I could past that

I was able to cool down and still felt the shade

But let's call a spade a spade

With God's due diligence

My people and I knew this would eventually all fade.

I understand it all better like it was a video game system once I played.

No documentation and nothing was displayed

Had to pray and wait it out day by day.

It was like awaiting judgement day for that for final say.

God knew what was best to P.R.E.V.A.I.L

Sending messages that would stick to me like the saying from

AOL, "You got mail."

I will say that I'm thankful and appreciative.

Now that it's all set and done with me

Learning a valuable lesson in which I'm in
Position to share and give.
I left my loft to enjoy the song of the soft
sounding lyrics from "Movin' on Up"
Head up as I do the famous walk with my queen
and be prepared to talk!

Last Kiss

Thinking back with thoughts of uncontrollable events

Several shots but not several attempts

One left for thinking

While third eye at the moment blinking.

I apologize but I stood my ground

You crossed the line and was out of bounds

Altercation resulting in warning sounds

I dreamed about that moment but

refused to be lost and found.

I know some are waiting for me to expound

but I put it all in God's hands.

Eyes on me while my loved ones were watching

as if they're in the stands

I refuse to be dealt with like Judas

Blindly betrayed by a Brutus

And I won't let a Delilah do me like Sampson

But unfortunately, it involved my son

I prayed and repent

Everything was orchestrated and heaven sent

Sacrificed like it was lent

Longer than expected

Faith in God always keep us protected

Abundance of Blessings projected

"SEVENFOLD"

Confidence solid like pure gold

Ignorance is bliss

Redemption is my last kiss

Sons 2 Suns

When you'd see me and my son—
that was my identifier
Redemption was already prepared by God
to be placed in the air fryer.
I kept it all the way real—
never wanted to be a liar.
No need for that, lessons learned
Like a pinky promise and shoes being tied.
Dry eyed but
Every time I thought everything through,
It led to several moments in which I cried.
I'm still alive but away from you.
Hoping you don't think of me as if I died.
Praying the things I taught resonated.
When it came to raisin' you in the sun

Challenges like life's showers,

I never hesitated.

You've seen me do it alone

and now you get to see me with

a queen I'm blessed I dated.

She's been a true rider through storms

While carrying our son.

I feel true unconditional love

Through the air like a heaven-sent dove.

To you my son and my other son,

being together brings happiness

that lights a smile up brighter than the sun.

Involuntary Fight

I will never forget being locked in that cage,
Trapped in the cell, body filled with rage
Feenin' for that triple p,
That's my purpose, paper, and pen.
It gets deeper every time you turn the page.
Preparing for my next book...
Chocking each reader up
as they turn slowly while reading.
Feeling each word having them shook.
Sparring with words
As I jab and give right hooks.
Setting me up for my haymaker
Which is verbally and visually hitting kids
In the heart
Bringing them back to head start.
Don't forget I'm a giver and not a taker

Contradiction in a good way
While being a disciplinarian and heart breaker.
It's all for the good.
Even though I left,
I still do it for the hood.
Call the people and hit me with neglect.
Many are called
but few are chosen.
With that being said,
I feel when I was born,
My name was called so
God appointed and pressed select.
Purpose driven so we do what the
Most High expects.

King and Queen

A man who finds his queen has already found his best friend through an unconditional journey. That queen exemplifies love and strength through her experiences to being resilient. She's built to recognize her potential king as he enters her life. He may have been playing games like hide and go seek for years. A true king and queen know their value and worth. They may have settled for less than what they deserve in the past, but they've grown over the years. They settle for less due to falling in love with the potential of who that person can be rather than the person they truly are. The king and queen are pure and should be treasured. A king and queen deserve the world and everything in it. They are treasured more when they come together in which forms an ace. Their power together becomes one. Their strength together can get them through any challenge life may bring. They can build an empire from their foundation of love, trust, loyalty, communication, and other keys to a relationship. They have all the keys needed to open every door filled with opportunities.

Truth be told, sometimes one may have to go through things to see who's really there for them. It's sad but it seems like your queen or king is by your side at some of the lowest points of your life. Think about this and reflect a little on your own life. A queen and king are supposed to uplift one another. Both should be able to give and receive. It should not be one giving and the other just receiving. This is for all aspects of the relationship such as emotionally, financially, sexually, and etc. One should not be doing it all. As the saying goes, "It takes teamwork to make the dream work." Think about how teamwork is together and dream work is separate. This is an example of two becoming one in the pursuit to helping one another fulfill each other's dream or purpose.

With everything being said, I'm blessed to have found my queen. It has honestly been a tough journey, but I've always kept faith through it all. The power of prayer is real. My mom used to always say, "ask and you shall receive." When parents or grandparents say or do things. Trust and believe they be knowing. My mom's photo for when I call is of my queen and I side by side. I've been doing what momma always said which was praying and asking for everything I want and need but I believe God wanted me to wait. I had to finish going through things on my own. Once I've gone through everything, then God was ready to bless me. As my queen once told me as I cried like a baby in her arms. "As Newton's Law works, sometimes things have to shift in order for something else to come in." My life was like a cycle of just taking care of my son, working, and paying bills. I honestly didn't have much room for anything else. My journey has been a lot and for those who've supported and followed me already understand. Those who truly care for me will be really happy. Others who are in their feelings will probably despise or look at me different. I understand everyone will not be happy for me. I pray God will give them a change of heart to understand one day. I guess

God made room in my life by revealing who my queen was. I remember plenty of times just holding one another and crying. I was able to smile because I witness light underneath the tunnel. I tell her every chance I get but this woman is special. As Gucci Mane will say in *The Gucci Mane Guide to Greatness*, "Pay attention to women, they are brilliant. Listen closely to whoever the woman in your life is. She's a genius. She's watching you. You're important to her. If you've got a woman that feels like you're important to her, she must talk to you and communicate with you. Nine times out of ten, it's not to your detriment. It is to your benefit." These words speak volume to me and everything he's saying is true. My queen is beautiful and super intelligent. She's not perfect but she's the full package. She brings it all to the table which make me smile and turn me on. We know tables turn but our table is cemented and unable to turn based on our foundation. They say iron sharpen iron. My queen keeps me sharp in all areas. She even got my sneaker game on point. She's trying to low key turn me into a sneaker-head, but I must admit she has style. Her style is unorthodox and unmatched. They say a way to a man's heart is through his stomach. With that having been said, she can cook too. She literally got to my heart through her heart and mind. I can write a book on my queen, but you get the gist. Gucci ended a chapter off by saying "If you're fortunate to have a brilliant woman in your life, by your side or as your wife, be sure to listen to her." My queen has been with me through my journey, and I love her for that. As I look around in bed, the courtroom, the room of my speeches, and other places, all I see is my beautiful queen motivating me as I motivate others. A king and queen holding hands on a journey through *Love*, *Pain*, and *Glory* to **P.R.E.V.A.I.L**!

QUEEN/SOULMATE

Dear Lovanda,

God placed you, beautiful QUEEN, into my life.

I found a great one who I can grow with and one day make my wife.

I could've settled for anyone, but I had my eyes on you.

I've trusted the process, so I was patiently waiting for you.

Hints and signals on our journey finally went through.

"Thank You" for being my inspiration and motivation.

A piece of my heart in quotations.

I've played my cards; I've played chess.

Most importantly, I've prayed knowing God always blesses.

You're resilient and a genius.

We both share the same mother, Venus.

Us Against the World and All Eyes on Us.

Air Libra and Earth Taurus.

One card in hand—last!

Nowhere to go but up—checkmate!

Not only did I find my QUEEN,

but my

SOULMATE!

Love,

Leo

Book Love

Seduced by the way your cover look.

I love to put my hands on your book.

I love to turn you over from the front and back

Foreplay scene, first act.

Excited and aroused to open you up.

I love to observe each line below first and work my way up.

I love to lay you down and stand you up on my bed.

I love to be alone in my head.

I love to be in the moment and live each line.

Arching your back and holding onto your spine.

I'm so deep into you that I don't want to let go.

Even during the moment of awe which may seem like a no.

I love to keep my bookmark in the middle

just in case I have to quickly go.

I'm really into you so let me change positions so I won't get too fatigued.

Right there, as you take over my body and mind

with a mouth dropping scene that has me so intrigued

A moment of silence as I close my eyes

to feel your poetic tongue and hear your words of enchantment.

Pure literary enhancement.

So descriptive and erotic that the cat got my tongue,

I must admit you got it.

Feeling the love making with flashes of ecstasy.

You're giving me self-help through fantasy.

You're a goddess of a writer,

Through every twist and turn, you're exotic.

I might just pull an all-nighter.

I love when I'm thumbing through you.

I love to hold you close as I'm coming on you.

I'm finished for now, but I'll be back

to open you up again for the second act.

The Moment

Through a man's accomplishment,

they say there's an influence of a woman's love.

I concur, whole-heartedly, with the statement mentioned above.

My journey was an experience,

filled with mixed emotions in which

was fulfilled by love and devotion.

I understood the pain that came within,

But the love and glory overshadowed and dismissed

all fears and ill-feelings that was embedded within.

The truth be told:

I've grown from all my lessons and God has guided

my every step on the journey and has rewarded me with

an abundance of Blessings.

The work that I've put in has gone unnoticed,

But it's nothing like a woman's true love for a man

and for who he is and his potential

which is all noticed.

I've waited my turn,

But always had faith that my queen will one day return.

Each move was a tough move

But I believed God wanted me overtime to improve.

The moment,

she picked me off the ground and held my hand.

I just couldn't quite grasp the moment,

which was a blurred for my vision to understand.

I found her,

in the process of building self.

I didn't recognize her presence until I

completely found myself.

I found a good thing.

Love, Pain, and Glory: Redemption

glorifies moments of love

revealed between a Queen and a King.

God has shown me that the saying is true:

"Behind every great man, is a great woman."
The moment you think and build together
is the moment you both become one.

The moment you understand
That love and faith together
Will always lead you to believe
That you've already won.

Di Pree

First comes trust, then comes love.

Then the poking of the bear starts.

Reflecting from that test.

Show that you're superior and have it all above.

When it comes to love, they're so eager to feel your strength.

Challenge after challenge,

display your deepest wavelength.

Layer after layer,

Resides your deepest purpose.

Being poked might feel like it's being done on purpose.

Exotic moment when you display divine masculine which is called "shiva"

She might nick pick with you

And be extra like a diva.

It's all coming from the feminine love at the end of the day.

So don't take it personal with everything they say.

They say the most loving women is the women that will test you.

Make a mistake and that's the moment they correct you.

Write your story and I promise you they're going to edit it.

Working together as a team that's how you credit it.

Once the foundation is established then it becomes accredited.

Two hearts, heads, and mouths are better than one.

Four eyes, ears, legs, arms, and hands are better than two.

Twenty toes are better than ten.

Do the math and understand the pree

It's proven and deep like one plus one equals three.

Stepping Out the Game

I was never a playa,
more like a lover.
Trying to save certain females.
Felt like Captain Save a Hoe or Casanova.

Gave my all
but in return got the cold shoulder.
Felt like a dog the way I bent her over.
Pound after pound
round after round.
The stroke is right
When you hear the mac and cheese sound.
Taking out my anger
Trying to break her wall down.
Treat her like a Domino
the way she falls down.

I pick her up
and then I do it all again.
Got her calling out of work
or calling up a friend.
Leave both doors wide open
because I'm coming in.

Retire my jersey
I'm stepping out the game

Some females like dogs
Some females like cats
You don't have to worry
I'm not judging based off that.
I'm trying to hit a homerun
When I'm up at bat
If I hit and only land on base
Just know I'm sliding in

hoping I don't cum on your face.

These were a few of my bachelor highlights.
Now that I'm considered a Master of life
I've already faced the flashing lights.
I'm now in the Love of Fame
I had my share of fun with several woman
Now I'm stepping out the game.

Retire my jersey
I'm stepping out the game

True poet,
but some people don't acknowledge it.
I refuse to debate parties,
I'm not a politician
Almost caught in the system
but God got me out it.

I gave my whole life

far from a little bit.

Life moving so fast

God will make you sit.

Rethink your entire life

and have you come up with a legitimate plan.

Have you achieve all your goals,

so the world can understand.

Thanks to all my believers

You're my biggest fans.

P.R.E.V.A.I.L #7,

Hang my jersey in the stands.

Mine

-with Lovanda Brown

(*Lovanda Brown*)

As fate would have it

You've seen me long before

I held you in view

You've known me long before

I accepted knowing you

And as you waited,

You left our fate in the hands of time

Now today I know that I am yours and

you,

my love,

are mine.

You've held strong each time

I looked the other way,

And was there to direct my vision

Knowing exactly what to say,

And with your full awareness

of all the ties that bind

I became yours and you, inevitably,

Became mine.

I don't know what's to come

And you know where I fall short.

When words fail to meet my lips,

You're there to help me sort,

Through all the thoughts I have of you,

Meanwhile, struggling to see

That I, indeed was made for you

and you were meant for me!

As fate would have it,

our stars met and with courage-

they've aligned,

We've stood to follow their direction:

Hands laced and hearts intertwined,

And because now I know

the hardened heart

is what Love seeks to find,

Because of you I now know-

I am yours and

You're forever...

Mine."

(Leo James)

First time speaking to you,

You came across firm but sweet

So I'm thinking,

"Now or Later"

God knew us coming together as one

was the plan for the greater.

I've always believed that life gets greater later

Our first conversation was strictly business

but I knew you could relate

I've learned on our journey to enjoy what's
right on my plate.
The introduction at Starbucks was
an unknowingly first date
God took my hand and lead me to fate.
My mom still has that picture of us for
Every time when I call.
I knew your heart was big when you told
me I was tall
You looked up to me and at the same
time I looked up to you.
My words make everything seem so perfect.
But only if some really knew what we been
through.
First Introduction, then came The Last Tears,
Redemption is right here.
We both knew that life didn't fight fair.

But we had to fight fear and show that we both cared.

A journey filled with Love, Pain, and Glory

that we both shared.

All di proof lead mi fi believe,

You're mine.

The power of words can be rewind to

Know I have your back as you look back at

me ah do di dutty wine.

Despite all that we've encountered,

You,

my love,

are Mine!

Couples Therapy

Redemption is here,

Deep into the soul,

Time to take couples there.

When it comes to falling in love,

It's normal to be scared,

But hard times will get you prepared.

No relationship is perfect.

For every action, there's a reaction.

Like cause and effect.

Our love language may be off

or explicit.

Forcing unnecessary arguments

No need to get specific

Through ups and downs,

Thick and thin,

Hard and good times,

Until death do you apart

Thinking finish at the moment

but don't forget about the start.

Restore all the great memories

found inside the heart.

The grass isn't always greener on the other side

We tend to forget about those moments

of ride or die.

Now we're ready to flee and take flight,

only to land alone.

Freeze, fight, and flight

due to the known versus the unknown.

Remember that better days will soon come.

Think everything through before you decide to run

Don't allow emotions to divide you two

To become one vs one

God gives His toughest battles to His strongest soldiers.

Together while fulfilling God's purpose, you both will P.R.E.V.A.I.L and overcome all adversity and opposition.

Keep each other intact filled with confidence and ambition.

It should be all eyes on you two

Against The World,

No friendly competition.

Don't bring in jealousy and greed

Point, blank, period.

Mood swings will lead the relationship to bleed,

Out of control

But don't be controlled by the love for a dollar bill

That's banking on a fast way to withdraw

and let the relationship go down hill

When love is real,

the pain within

shouldn't be difficult to heal.

Despite hard times,

be willing to plead or appeal

Love is not a game,

Like deal or no deal

When 2 comes together to become ONE,

The love multiplies

And becomes 4real!

Chance

Everyone deserves a chance to show that they're capable to achieve whatever they put their mind to. I remember the day vividly during my sophomore year in high school. It was spring football, and I was watching my high school team practice because my sister's boyfriend played on the team. I noticed the team preparing for the special team's portion of practice. So, I asked my sister, "do you think I should try out?' She looked at me and said, "it's up to you." At that moment, I was contemplating on if I was ready to make that sacrifice. For those who know me know that I can be very indecisive at times. Something within told me to go ahead and take that chance. So I ran home as if I was Forrest Gump to grab my shorts and soccer cleats. I jumped over the field fence and ran up to the coach and my soon-to-be fellow teammates. They all looked at me and each other like "where did this kid come from." It was a random moment but a moment to show others what I can offer. The head coach stared at me with an unsure looked and said, "how do I know that you can kick kid?" I smiled with extreme confidence and responded with a typical kid response. "Let me show you." One teammate hiked the ball to the other teammate as he placed it down on the tee with the laces facing the goal post. With all eyes on me, I put my head down and kicked the ball as we watched the ball fly through the uprights. The coached looked at me with a smile which seemed more like a grin and said, "You're on the team kid." That moment was a chance given to where I could have been denied. I was officially apart of the Hillhouse football team. We lost in the state championship game my freshman year, that fact made it special when I became a part of the redemption team. We ended up winning the state championship and it was one of the greatest feelings in the world. I remember the head coach holding up the newspaper sports section of the lost from the following year. During the half time speech, he ripped up the article, and said "let's go out there and kick their fucking ass." Our team was hyped and prepared to bring the championship home. Everything came together from the beginning to the day we all received our state championship rings. The head coach gave many of the players their own personal introduction to receiving their rings. The head coached recited the same spring football story that I shared with you all as he said my name to everyone applauding and clapping. I finished my football career with a state championship ring, First-Team All-Area, Third Team All-State, First Team All-Levi Jackson Team, Sam Masko Special Teams award, and Scholar-Athlete of the Year Award. Many people used to laugh at me on just being a kicker, but I never paid it any attention. I knew my position and place on the team. I let my awards and accolades speak for itself. I was blessed and given a chance to put my head down, kick my feet up and put my hands up because I know it's all good.

Blacked Out

Walking like I'm on black ice.

Bounced back after slipping.

I'm always locked down in writer's mode,

so I'm never tripping.

I've cooked up a 3-course meal

so I'm getting out the kitchen.

Writer's block couldn't stop me.

I just thought I should mention.

Talib Kweli, Black Thought, and I

share the same birthday.

We all tip our pen like the Libra scale

so that alone is a lot to say.

I'm confident that I'm amongst

the great writers of today.

Imagine if I rapped, I'll probably have more respect

but instead, I'm writing books and speaking to crowds.

My words would be hitting on beats

like the boom box with the cassette.

I wonder if people felt my greatness

the first time that we met.

Put your money on me now that I'll shake a room.

I promise I won't let you down so place your bet.

I need a great introduction to when I'm walking out.

Journey was a marathon that felt like a race.

Now I'm on stage blacked out.

Down and Up

I used to walk around with my head down,

Now it's up.

I been through things that tried to put me down,

I leveled up.

I fell down hard but I couldn't stay down,

I rosed up.

I watched my brothers cross the line for a touchdown,

One finger up.

I was called in the game with my head down,

My foot is up.

Follow through when they put the ball down,

It's good, hands up.

I put my all in it when I push down,

So I push up.

My pen in my hand as I write down,

Until I finish up.

My legacy is cemented and stamped down,

Look it up.

3 book journey with this one down,

My time with poetry is up.

Law of Attraction

Dealing with the pain could leave you
mentally and physically drained.
Keeping God first, you could always feel the love.
Feeling like you're drowning
the faith will help keep your head above.
Deep thought mixed with a burning desire
will have you purpose driven and prepared to inspire.
Think rich, grow rich mindset
is your own will power set on the mind.
You master your own thoughts once you
become a master of your own mind.
Knowledge is power so allow your mind to
meditate and soak in words that shower.
Whatever you want then just reach and go get it.

Whatever you want to be then just act it and be it.

All great leaders were dreamers.

So with that being said,

you must envision it in order to see it.

Be like a kid and use your imagination.

Put your dreams into action.

All these skills are a part of the law of attraction.

Put it out to the universe and watch it all manifest.

Watch how God work and give you an abundance of Blessings

with you as a walking testimony to attest.

It's a secret that can make you stand out from the rest.

Exert that energy from within and watch how it flow out.

You've been preparing and planning behind closed doors

so it all comes naturally when it's time to show out.

Being rich in spirit is aligned with being righteous.

Doing God's work is a sacrifice but it's priceless.

Give jewels for free and tell yourself that you're the nicest.

Selfish people will take your kindness for weakness.

So use your strength to applying pressure

to make more diamonds to display your uniqueness.

Growth

Fact is that there are skills you lack
Have to focus on the future.
Can't let the mind go back.
If it does, use autosuggestion
To get you back on track.

Close your eyes, just envision
all positive thoughts.
You're in control
so master your thoughts.

Don't let this cruel world
alternate your thinking.
It could happen so quickly,
the same way as blinking.

Just stay on course as you do good deeds.
Cleanse your mind, heart, and soul
like a period cycle
as it cries and bleeds.
Keep faith and share love
and watch God fulfill all needs.

God will do things on purpose
until you feel a burning desire.
Force you to sit down *write* there
So you can be prepared to inspire.

All great leaders had to learn
a valuable lesson.
Mental scars from that time
of stressing.
Pay the price but it will turn
to a Blessing.

That's the time,

you build your confidence and take control.

Not knowing, but at the same time

you're achieving a special goal.

That's significant growth

leading you to play your role.

Ready, Set, Go!

The Resolve

They're thinking who are you?

Because they don't know who the person on a mission is

Let them know straight up

It's all for the kids

P.R.E.V.A.I.L is a lifestyle

A culture that we live

It's not about what we take

But what we give.

Going headfirst with manuscript after manuscript.

So we're prepared

and never scared.

Can't just be talking

because actions speak louder than words.

Everything mentioned are facts and not just rhyming words.

On my journey I left quotes and key words.
Plenty of deep lines to decode and signs
for one's own journey road.
My own dream where some may think
was extreme.
Blessings through it all is what I redeem.
With that all being said,
Redemption is a part of the glory stage.
You're only as good as your last move.
Let that resonate before turning the page.

Hear Me Save You

Technology enslaving you.

Tic Tok keep clicking.

One dance for the man

can't possibly save you

Tic tock goes the time wasted

Whole time you didn't even realize you

could've possibly made it

Posting selfies on Facebook and looking

Hoping for an elite management booking

Posing for followers on Instagram

Whole show for an audience who didn't give a damn

Hope they told you to spend quality time with your fam

Got a hopeful still waiting on a

social media ban

Secret agendas got our minds stuck in a box

We are living in the matrix and focused on ROBLOX

Technology leading to self-destruction.

Kids, today, can't see the true value in self construction.

All while falling in Mortal Kombat's fatality.

Different ways to keep you locked in-they call it virtual reality.

Do the floss with your teeth each night.

Reward really comes after doing things right.

Get locked in and lose sleep with your purpose-Fortnite

Stop following and start your own

Challenge by leading

which will lead to one actually succeeding.

I know it's all fun and games but show

Respect to your elders and not be rude.

Subscribe to your calling and watch it all play out,

That's You-Tube.

Don't fall for the trap

And get stuck in the moment like

"Oh snap"

Try calling instead of texting at times to chat.

People will go ghost on you real quick like SnapChat.

Do what you want to do but I just want to advise you.

Pay attention to what you absorb.

Don't let the media change your core.

I just hope one day that this will resonate as true

Just a young hopeful praying you

help me save you.

Only the Beginning

Today is a new day
Waking up is a Blessing.
Success feels like
One is going astray.
Some people are stagnant
so they just want you to stay.
Have to level up when you
aiming for the stars.
Think about the time you struggle
It left a lot of scars
Try not to look back
when trying to go far.
Stare in the mirror and reflect,
I know you see that shining star.

Sometimes you see the ending in the beginning

Birth come to mind which symbolize winning

New beginning allows you to be reborn

and strive for what your heart desire

You have the ability to calm a storm

and put out any given fire.

Your journey won't be smooth like ice

cream but expect rocky road.

You will always have dirty laundry

but handle it with success load by load.

Remember to never quit and give life your all.

It's you who will lead the way

So stand and be ready to answer the call.

Tell yourself: "Failure is not an option so I will not fail.

This is only the beginning and I—WILL—P.R.E.V.A.I. L!

Please Read

Yes, I'm begging and pleading on my hands and knees

Please read just knowing that money don't grow on trees

Don't waste knowledge and wisdom giving for free

or a meal full of words giving in three

Reading is Fun-Da-Mental

All of my Love, Pain, and Glory will be Monu-Mental

Breaking things down

of pure lyricism without an instrumental.

I may look like a rapper

which I hear during every speech

but I strive to make my audience feel and envision my words

while I preach and teach.

Reading seems to go extinct

The love of literature has been indistinct.

People nowadays don't like to analyze and think

Libraries might all shut down

So there won't be a place to read and sit down

Some will say Barnes and Noble

but technology has taken over due to our obsession with our mobile

Please read books but if not that at least our rights

To be woke is for our brains to release informational lights

Don't trust anyone who don't have a bookcase

Be that one to be banking with wisdom and knowledge like Chase

Please stop listening all the time and read

Writers write to quietly lead

Love, Pain, and Glory is like a bible story for the youth

Even one can reveal their own truth.

Look up bread and circuses,
while thinking about the saying:

"If you entertain a clown,

you become a part of the circus."

Do you get it?

Please read because I promise it's worth it!

Story

We were born in the world

to open arms of love.

To be or not to be?

Read it again

While thinking about your own life

In between, and above.

Pain creeps in and changes things.

Trauma is what it brings.

Unfinished business is a legit business

Especially when those involved

haven't opened up for dialogue and forgiveness.

Glory is a celebration of an

accomplishment from one's story.

Put it all together and then you have a tale.

You can give it out for free or for sale.

They say a story shouldn't be told but sold

So please don't leave this world

with a greatest story untold.

The Greatest

All praise goes to God because I wouldn't be where I'm at if it wasn't for those several blessings and opportunities. I take pride in being the greatest in whatever I put my mind to. I was destined to be great since I came into this world. I know based off the hard work I put in that I was a great soccer player, football player, student, friend, son, dad, poet, author, and the list continues. I'm writing this in a humbling way because I've also known that all these things required sacrifice and a struggle. I heard in order for someone to master something, they will need to put in 10,000 hours. That's the amount of time that one should be working on their craft in order to master it. Some may agree and disagree but I mean each is own. The point is to continue to grind and put in the work to be the greatest at whatever you set your mind to. My purpose is to be a Motivational Speaker for our youth and anyone in need. I'm very passionate in speaking to others. I love to motivate and guide others on their personal journey. I've

learned that every human is different. I've
learned the difference between people who are
kinesthetic, visual, and auditory. I had to
prepare and come up with creative ways to
deliver messages that will touch the three
types of people. I put out to the universe that I
will be one of the greatest motivational
speakers in the world. God heard me and put
me in position to be just that. I'm still doing
my research and homework. I still recall
telling one of my older brothers, "I'm going to
be one of the greatest motivational speakers in
the world." He looked at me and said, "bro you
will need to go through more things than what
you've gone through." I responded back like a
typical young kid, "but bro I have gone
through enough." I felt really discouraged but
now I understand what he meant. I've been on
a mission ever since to be one of the greatest
motivational speakers. My main audience is
our youth because they need more guidance.
When I was going to school, we had people
come and talk to the kids. It doesn't seem like
the schools and programs do that nowadays.
I'm determined to bring that back because our
kids need it. They need hope and to see more
people that look just like them who have

experienced the same or similar upbringing. Our kids are being sold false hope. Throughout all my speeches, I always manage to deliver nothing but real. I want them to see and feel everything I'm saying. The ultimate goal is to give them opportunity to make money, build confidence, a resume, and other positive outlets provided. The youth need something to believe in that's concreate and pure assurance. These things are what inspired me to create the P.R.E.V.A.I.L Youth Empowerment Organization. I personally put P.R.E.V.A.I.L on hold to build myself up which was sharing my journey of Love, Pain, and Glory. I wanted my family, community, and the world to know who I am completely and what I bring to the table. We all know money is the ultimate starting factor. But I believed my vision will accrue money and support from our communities. It just made it hard to work, pay bills, and try to make this vision become a reality. I let go and let God who's giving me the strength in aligning everything together. The youth and their families need that genuine support. I look forward to building our boys and girls to women and men and then to recognize their highest divine level as kings and queens. They will be equipped with the skills needed to be self-reliant and self-employed. P.R.E.V.A.I.L reflects who I am and what success is. It's a lifestyle I've adapted and been living since I've curated it.

Celebrate

I've grown up as that lost seed left in the soil.

Get pushed to the point

where your temper starts to boil.

You can tell I'm around

By the smell of my oil.

No matter the situation

just always remain focus.

I studied psychology

and I understand how it could be a little hocus-pocus.

I don't mind as long as I have a degree.

I study the mind so we could agree to disagree.

As long as we could come to an understanding

And no one is being too demanding.

Exchanging words but not like we're

doing hand to hand combat

Stimulating one another's mind

is as simple as that

no argument but a debate or intellectual conversation.

Surprising one another like the form of revelation.

Anything lost can be found again except for time wasted so

the time to build through words is worth it.

Champagne to celebrate.

Cheers go ahead and pour it.

The Glory is here as we're sitting at the table,

Metaphorically for standing at the finish line.

I gave you a 3-course writing meal,

So let us bow our heads and say our grace

since its dinner time.

Amen!

God is My Judge

(Chorus)

God is my judge

No one else can judge me (2x)

God is my judge,

That's who I'm waiting for.

Praying day and night

With my knees on the floor.

I'm being patient while I'm waiting

for that open door.

God said I'm not done

Son, I have some more.

Just a few more lessons to learn.

What I've been through,

I've had to take the chosen journey

before my breakthrough.

Motivating all my people
and educating too.
Praying hands celebrating
while I bust a move.
It's a slow dance with light kicks.
All praise goes to God,
In which I've did it in advance.

God is my judge
No one else can judge me (2x)

I was waiting on God
when the devil wanted to play.
Trying to take my soul
Hoping I have nothing to say
trying to catch me slipping while
I'm at my lowest point.

Not knowing I'm anointed and running point.

I call shots plus I'm a playmaker.

I signed a contract with God,

I'm not a deal breaker.

Every time I say my prayer,

I say my soul to keep.

When I share Love, Pain, and Glory.

Best believe it's deep.

Everyone is going to feel it

from their head, heart, and feet.

Remember that God is our judge,

So Glory to any defeat!

God is my judge

No one else can judge me (2x)

God is My Glory

I took a different path,

I decided to be a writer.

The journey was long, but we stuck it out

like a freedom rider.

Now that I said what I said, and I'm done.

I'm prepared to speak to my people.

Let me start.

So let me wash my hands off first

In order to feed you.

A sacrifice from God was needed

In order to really reach you.

My journey not too far-fetched.

Love, Pain, and Glory.

Artistic with my words so you can see

what I sketched.

Then I've drawn it up in which was all

a part of the plan.
P.R.E.V.A.I.L made me this inspiring man.
Doing God's work on Godspeed.
Going back daily to nurture each seed.
One hand washes the other, so I was
willing to throw in my hand.
I pray that you truly understand.
God's my everlasting light.
Main reason why I shine bright
every time I write.
God is my source as I cite
when sharing my story.
All the Blessings I received was giving as
a receipt that God is my Glory.

Spotlight

Future so bright
That I see it from a clear view.
Sometimes from a bird's eye view.
Life is a test
That I always have to review.
I have a study partner now.
She's my study guide.
We build one another up.
That's how we coincide.
I can't be stagnant
so I prefer to be in overdrive.
Since my soccer days
I've always had a fast strive.
Chris Webber of my brothers.
Call us the Fab Five.
Wrong moment when I called timeout.
Made perfection like Hov in Reasonable Doubt.

Illmatic mindset like Nas, I'm a game changer.

It's funny how you get more love sometimes from a stranger.

Redemption is officially an end to my run from poetry.

Trilogy of my life, allow you to get to know me openly.

They say death come in threes

but it's resurrection to me for the world to see.

That's the moment you become free and amazing.

If you heard me say this,

then you would understand that's what I was always facing.

It felt like I was raised in.

Sorry if you don't understand what I was saying.

Focused was my attitude with P.R.E.V.A.I.L.

No portraying but always praying.

Prophecy

Rolling dice while playing Monopoly.

I pray our youth learn a lot from me.

Within 3 books, I instilled a legacy.

God's gift of a prophecy.

God is always by my side to watch me drive.

I was able to do something special while my parents are still alive.

Air sign so it was bound for me to fly.

No need for glasses when you have a 3rd eye.

20/20 vision but lost a few contacts.

Twenty-Twenty Won (2021) but still serving God's divine contract.

The devil tried its best to recruit me

Glory to God for setting me free.

After every test, I made some type of correction.

Time away and being alone made perfection.

Love, Pain, and Glory is a literary collection.

Reborn again during this time,

Call it resurrection.

It was hard but I made it happen.

Round of applause,

So feel and see the clapping.

Holding back but if the tears fall

then I'll just keep my head up while I'm standing tall.

Delivering messages and praying it

reaches you all.

Made It

All praise and glory to God because I made it.

If you followed my journey, then WE made it.

Prophesized life in words, it was all stated.

Now I think about times, some work should've been dated.

Love, Pain, and Glory is something we all can relate with.

After shedding last tears then redemption is what you bounce back with.

Trials and tribulations testing you through situations.

God put you through it, so you don't owe anyone explanations.

Some people don't like sharing much about themselves, so they only give a sample.

But my mission required more from me defining myself as a leader by example.

Far from being perfect but wasn't afraid to be judged.

I was willing to take chances in order to seek adequate change, so therefore I budged.

I decided to create my own path but consciously following the universe's math.

Astrology, numerology, psychology, theology, and the list goes on with the different branches of knowledge.

Always be willing to educate yourself with an open mind allowing yourself to or not to acknowledge.

Lessons are being giving and taught but keep in mind that some of the most valuable lessons cannot be brought.

You may be forced to learn on your own and overtime discover something unknown.

Think about what you want to be remembered for.

Whatever comes to mind then you will have to give more.

Think twice and be prepared to sacrifice.

A struggle will follow after, just a heart filled with words of advice.

That moment when you realize you made it,

You'll feel free as you say it,

"I made it!"

My Everything

My goal was to remain consistent when
my dreams allowed me to be persistent.

My plan was structured to be executed
and still rise like the rose deeply rooted.

My mind was trained to be able to distinguish
between consciousness and sub-consciousness.

My heart was lost, broken, and healed
as Love, Pain, and Glory revealed.

My love was shared in conditional and
unconditional ways

for all to help support them get through challenging days.

My pain was endured to help build my character and confidence

through the growing process in which I was able to maintain, lose, and gain.

My glory was acknowledged and celebrated for overcoming

so much adversity and creating the narrative to my story.

My time was invested in building a legacy and foundation

through deep words of genuine and pure motivation.

My purpose was P.R.E.V.A.I.L to inspire people in need of help especially the youth to understand their true existence through a gospel of truth.

P.R.E.V.A.I.L 4

"Why P.R.E.V.A.I.L 4"

Growing up,

I came a long way

From dirty houses and hallways.

Praying to God everyday

doing what the Lord say.

Fulfilling my purpose

Just living my dreams.

Not every nightmare

is as dark as it seems

God always come through

When we're in need for

some light.

I got my two sons

So I know I'm going to

Shine bright

"What's your real Purpose?

I took a left turn to that cell

So God sat me down

and made me write.

Thinking all along:

"P.R.E.V.A.I.L"

God chose me

So I chose our youth

Next book,

I'm prepared

To start revealing the truth

I saved the best for last

I have to stay on top

Like high school,

top boy of my class.

"Was you really setup?"

Minor setback for
Major comeback
All praise goes to God
for putting me in position
spoke things into existence
then it all came to fruition
on my hands and knees
crying
Feeling everything, I was wishing
It took many sacrifices
Just to be free and amazing
That's the powerful blessing of praying

"Do you think people are going to actually read?"

Redemption will open many eyes

To finally see what I was saying

They say if you ever want to hide something

from a nigga, just put It a book.

I ask you again to please read

While tapping into your 3rd eye

to analyze when you look

Read between the lines,

At least see the plot,

Whenever it's a trilogy,

Always expect a lot.

"Are you really done with poetry?"

Before I start speaking again,

Let's take a moment to pray.

"I introduced myself,

I shed my Last Tears,

I redeemed myself"

All filled with

"Love, Pain, and Glory"

There's nothing more left to say.

"What's your definition of Redemption?"

Twenty-Twenty felt like it won (2020-2021)

but in reality, Thirty-one, thirty actually won (31)!

I'm still standing, I'm still tall.

Redemption

Exemplifies the rise after the fall.

Your response when your name is called.

Leading by example and giving your all

Never let a situation define you

Keep in mind if you do one thing

They're ready to throw the book and judge you.

I've spoken and forever hold my piece

Love and Blessings to you all,

Peace!

THANK YOU

www.ingramcontent.com/pod-product-compliance
Lightning Source LLC
Chambersburg PA
CBHW030937090426
42737CB00007B/461